Scientists
IN ACTION

ENTOMOLOGISTS IN ACTION

CRABTREE
PUBLISHING COMPANY
WWW.CRABTREEBOOKS.COM

Anne Rooney

Author: Anne Rooney

Series research and development: Reagan Miller

Editorial director: Kathy Middleton

Photo research: James Nixon

Editors: Paul Humphrey, James Nixon, Ellen Rodger

Proofreader: Lorna Notsch

Designer: Keith Williams (sprout.uk.com)

Prepress technician: Samara Parent

Print coordinator: Katherine Berti

Layout: Keith Williams (sprout.uk.com)

Consultant: Brianne Manning

Produced for Crabtree Publishing Company
by Discovery Books

Cover image: An entomologist studies bugs at night

Photographs:

Alamy: pp. 4 (Nature Picture Library), 11 (Dino Fracchia),
18 (Les Gibbon), 19 bottom (Dino Fracchia), 20 top
(dpa picture alliance), 21 (Edwin Remsberg), 22 (XM
Collection), 23 (National Geographic Creative), 24
(ZUMA Press Inc), 25 (dpa picture alliance), 26 (ROPI).
Courtesy of Andrew Hammond: p. 17 top.
Shutterstock: pp. 7 top (Fotokostic), 7 middle left (jirasak_
kaewtongsorn), 7 middle right (Tyler Olson), 9 top (Elke
Kohler), 9 bottom (Sanimfocus), 10 (Forest man72),
12 (BEJITA), 13 top (Heiti Paves), 14 (Ramukanji), 16
(Khamkhlai Thanet), 17 bottom (Akos Nagy), 18 top
(Imfoto), 20 bottom (Song Pin), 27 (Littlekidmoment),
28 top (maxpro), 28 middle (Africa Studio), 28 bottom
(Labrador Photo Video), 29 (vitchuta thaithammakul).
Wikimedia: pp. 5 top (Keith Weller), 5 bottom (Tarmo
Lampinen), 6 bottom (Sharp Photography), 8 top
(Thomas Quine), 8 bottom, 13 bottom (Fábio Rodrigues
Pozzebom / AB), 15 (Peggy Greb), 19 top (Neil
Sanscrainte / U.S. Department of Agriculture).
All other images from Shutterstock

Library and Archives Canada Cataloguing in Publication

Rooney, Anne, author
        Entomologists in action / Anne Rooney.

(Scientists in action)
Includes index.
Issued in print and electronic formats.
ISBN 978-0-7787-5206-6 (hardcover).--
ISBN 978-0-7787-5217-2 (softcover).--
ISBN 978-1-4271-2158-5 (HTML)

        1. Entomologists--Juvenile literature. 2. Entomology--Juvenile
literature. I. Title.

QL467.2.R666 2018   j595.7   C2018-903003-8
                                           C2018-903004-6

Library of Congress Cataloging-in-Publication Data

Names: Rooney, Anne, author.
Title: Entomologists in action / Anne Rooney.
Description: New York, New York : Crabtree Publishing, 2018. |
    Series: Scientists in action | Includes index.
Identifiers: LCCN 2018033708 (print) | LCCN 2018039654 (ebook) |
    ISBN 9781427121585 (Electronic) |
    ISBN 9780778752066 (hardcover) |
    ISBN 9780778752172 (pbk.)
Subjects: LCSH: Entomology--Juvenile literature. | Entomologists--
    Juvenile literature.
Classification: LCC QL467.2 (ebook) | LCC QL467.2 .R662 2018 (print)
    | DDC 595.7--dc23
LC record available at https://lccn.loc.gov/2018033708

Crabtree Publishing Company
www.crabtreebooks.com   1-800-387-7650

Printed in the U.S.A./102018/CG20180810

Published in Canada
Crabtree Publishing
616 Welland Ave.
St. Catharines, Ontario
L2M 5V6

Published in the United States
Crabtree Publishing
PMB 59051
350 Fifth Avenue, 59th Floor
New York, New York 10118

Published in the United Kingdom
Crabtree Publishing
Maritime House
Basin Road North, Hove
BN41 1WR

Published in Australia
Crabtree Publishing
3 Charles Street
Coburg North
VIC, 3058

CONTENTS

A WORLD IN MINIATURE

Billions of locusts descend on a farm in Mexico. Within minutes, they've stripped the vegetation bare, eating their way through the farmer's crops and destroying the family's livelihood. A team of entomologists jump into action, collecting insects to examine in the lab. Locusts threaten crops around the world. They have caused famines (mass starvation) for thousands of years. Entomologists are investigating what causes locusts to swarm and destroy crops. They have found that locusts change their physical appearance and behavior just before they swarm. Can the entomologists find a way to stop swarms from forming?

Locust swarms contain a very large number of individuals, making it easy to catch specimens with a net.

What Is an Entomologist?

Entomologists are biologists who study arthropods, which are small, jointed creatures such as insects, spiders, and centipedes. Many entomologists explore how arthropods live and develop; others look at their impact on humans, other animals, plants, and the environment. Entomologists improve our knowledge of science in such areas as **evolution**, **ecology**, medicine, and **environmental science**. Like other scientists, entomologists follow the principles of science practice as they plan and carry out their investigations (see page 10).

What Are Arthropods?

Arthropods are invertebrates — animals with no backbone. All arthropods have a hard outer case rather than a skeleton made of bone inside them. Arthropods include insects, arachnids (such as spiders, scorpions, and **mites**), centipedes and millipedes, and **crustaceans**. Entomologists study land-based crustaceans, such as woodlice, but not those that live in water, such as crayfish and shrimp.

An entomologist experiments with a newly developed bait to trap cockroaches. These arthropods can cause disease in humans, and are hard to get rid of.

The caterpillar of the parsnip webworm is a pest that can destroy vulnerable parsnip crops.

From the Field: May Berenbaum

May Berenbaum is an American entomologist. She investigates plant-eating insects and the plants they eat. Her research shows how groups of plants and insects live and **evolve** together. She explores how plants protect themselves against specific arthropod pests, by making poisonous chemicals, for example, and how pests evolve to work around these defenses. She has found that when wild parsnip was introduced to North America around 1600, a pest that attacks it, parsnip webworm, was not carried with the plants. The parsnip's defense against webworm became unimportant. When the webworm arrived in America many years later, the plants had lost their chemical defense and were soon attacked by the pest.

ARTHROPODS ALL AROUND

There are more arthropods on Earth than any other type of creature. More than a million **species** have been described by entomologists—and there could be up to 10 times as many. Entomologists study all aspects of arthropods' lives and roles in **ecosystems**, and study them in all their stages from eggs to adults. They tackle important questions, such as:

- How can we prevent and treat diseases carried by arthropods?

- How can we keep important insects, such as bees, safe?

- How can we protect food crops and farm animals against pests, such as beetles and flies?

- How can we protect buildings against destructive insects, such as woodworm and **termites**?

- How are arthropods evolving and changing?

- How is **climate change** affecting where arthropods live?

- How many types of arthropods have not yet been investigated by entomologists? Where do they live, and what do they do?

Insects play essential roles in ecosystems. Dung beetles bury and recycle waste. This is good for the soil, and the removal of dung can prevent disease from spreading to animals such as cattle.

Why Arthropods Matter

Arthropods carry out essential tasks that keep the world running. They **pollinate** flowers, so that plants will make fruit and seeds. They break down natural waste, such as animal droppings and dead plants and animals. But they can also be a threat or nuisance. Some carry diseases that affect people, animals, or plants, and others feed on crops we grow. Entomologists find ways to use and protect helpful arthropods, and to reduce the harm other arthropods cause.

Farmers often spray crops with chemicals to destroy arthropod pests.

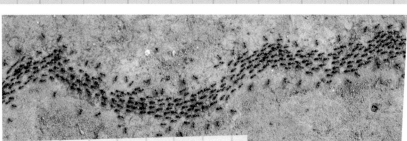

Insects that work together, such as ants, or fly in unusual ways inspire the designers of new technologies.

Learning from Insects

Research into insect bodies and behavior can help scientists progress in areas outside entomology. The way that ants find and use the shortest route between two points is used in designing telecommunications networks! Small robots used to search for survivors in collapsed buildings are designed with a similar body structure to that of cockroaches. Research into how flying insects hover has helped in the development of tiny drones.

Putting Science to Work

Entomologists work in many areas, from agriculture and medicine to forestry and **robotics**. For instance, medical entomologists identify and study arthropods that carry disease, and find ways to protect people from them. Crop-protection entomologists tackle arthropod pests. Ecological entomologists protect arthropods. Some research, such as discovering and describing more species of arthropods, is not directly useful to everyday life, but it extends our knowledge of science and may prove helpful in the future.

BUGS PAST AND PRESENT

People have always lived alongside arthropods and learned about useful ones, such as bees that make honey and silkworms that make silk. But until the invention of the microscope in around 1600, they could not see small **organisms** in great detail. Scientists studied the behavior and life cycles of arthropods while knowing little of how their bodies worked.

Collecting and Classifying

Arthropods are small and easy to collect. In the 1600s, **naturalists** and enthusiasts began to build collections from around the world. They **classified** the arthropods they found, grouping them by similarities in their bodies or behavior, and wrote the first books about them. Scientists still classify the new species of arthropods that are discovered every year.

Collections such as this display of butterflies are the product of careful and detailed work by early entomologists.

Living with Arthropods

At first, scientists focused on arthropods that were directly useful, such as silkworms, or troublesome arthropods, such as flies. In 1865, French biologist Louis Pasteur investigated a disease in silkworms, because it was costing the silk industry money. In 1897, British scientist Ronald Ross discovered that the disease malaria is carried by mosquitoes. This was the first time an arthropod had been linked with a human disease.

Louis Pasteur was the first person to investigate a disease in arthropods.

In the mid-1900s, powerful chemicals to kill arthropods, called pesticides, were developed. Unfortunately, they killed useful insects as well as pests and also harmed insect-eating animals.

Bees in Peril

A type of pesticide called nicotinoids still harms bees today. Bees are vital to our well-being, as they pollinate many crop plants. Entomologists try to find ways of controlling pests that destroy crops without harming useful insects. We need to do this to protect our food supply.

Some entomologists work to protect bees. Bees are essential to pollinating crops, such as rapeseed, a plant used to make cooking oil.

Saving a Continent

Thomas R. Odhiambo (1931–2003) was a Kenyan entomologist keen on developing science in Africa. He encouraged African entomologists to tackle human, animal, and plant diseases carried or caused by arthropods. His International Centre of Insect Physiology and Ecology (ICIPE) is still a center of excellence, attracting researchers from around the world. It focuses on insects that carry disease, such as the tsetse fly and mosquito, and the locusts that destroy crops. Odhiambo looked for inexpensive solutions that African farmers could use, preferring to manage pests through biological control rather than pesticides. Biological control uses natural organisms to kill pests. One example is introducing wasps from Pakistan to eat caterpillars that destroy corn in Kenya.

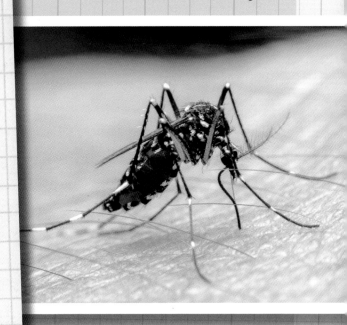

Entomologists study the complex process by which mosquitoes can pass on diseases and try to find methods of controlling them.

INVESTIGATING LIFE

All scientists structure their work in a similar way, even in very different fields. Entomologists are no exception; they begin their investigations by asking a question they want to answer.

Science Practices

Investigations in science involve the following practices:

- Asking questions
- Developing methods of investigation, including building **models** and designing observations and experiments
- Carrying out investigations
- Analyzing and interpreting **data** collected
- Using mathematics and technology to process data
- Constructing explanations from evidence
- Communicating findings and conclusions

Step by Step

Scientists design an investigation to collect data to answer the question they have asked. The investigation can involve experiments, or observations, or both. It might take place in the field—in the arthropods' natural **habitat**—or in the laboratory, or both. Arthropods can live anywhere, from a tropical rain forest to the coat of a dog, or a warehouse, so entomologists can find themselves working in all kinds of locations and conditions. Scientists need to be adaptable and resourceful, as an investigation may not always go as planned.

The data collected are just a starting point. Scientists have to analyze and interpret the data, carry out calculations, compare their data with other data, and sometimes, use computers to make predictions. The results lead scientists to conclusions or explanations.

These entomologists are gathering data by examining the arthropods living in a stream.

The Metric System

All entomologists use the metric system of measurements. Using the same units makes it very easy for scientists around the world to work together and to share and compare results.

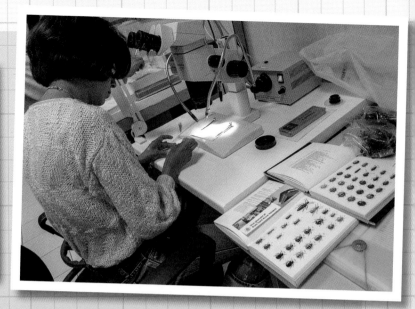

Back in the lab, entomologists identify the species of arthropods collected in the field.

Science in Progress

All scientists share and discuss their findings with their peers, other scientists working in the same field. This cooperative approach leads to the most reliable conclusions and helps science to progress. The results of one project often lead to new questions and new investigations. For example, finding that the population of a particular insect has increased might lead to a new investigation asking whether the population of a predator, an animal that eats the insect, has decreased.

From the Field: Stylianos Chatzimanolis

Stylianos Chatzimanolis of the University of Tennessee at Chattanooga looks for new species of rove beetles—a type of beetle with short wing-cases. While many entomologists hunt for new species in the field, Chatzimanolis investigates by looking through historical collections in museums. Rove beetles first appeared 220 million years ago. Chatzimanolis studies their evolution by looking at fossils. Many museums hold large collections of arthropods that have never been closely examined and described, and they provide a great opportunity to discover new species.

ASKING QUESTIONS OF THE WORLD

Entomologists ask questions about the lives, behavior, and **biology** of arthropods, and where they are found, or their distribution. Many look into how arthropods affect humans, in ways that are good or bad.

Problems and Pests

Entomologists looking at arthropod pests ask questions about those that feed on crops, trees grown for timber, or garden plants. Some arthropods cause damage in their adult form, such as aphids (greenfly) and locusts. Others are harmful in their **larval** stage— the caterpillars of many butterflies and moths damage crops. Some arthropods act as **vectors**, meaning that they carry a disease. **Microbes** or tiny **parasites** that cause disease are carried in or on the arthropods' bodies.

Termites destroy wood and can cause serious damage to buildings and other structures.

Broad and Narrow Questions

Some questions have a broad focus, such as "How will the distribution of arthropods that carry diseases alter with climate change?" Other questions are very specific. For example, an entomologist might examine how a certain type of insect carries a particular disease.

From the Field: Aqeel Ahmad

Aqeel Ahmad studies microbes inside insects that can make people sick. He collected flies from pig farms in the USA and took microbes from their gut. He found that the insects carried microbes that can cause food poisoning in humans. Some of the bacteria had become resistant to the medicines we use against them, or antibiotics. This means the antibiotics no longer kill the bacteria. Giving farm pigs antibiotics has led to the bacteria developing **resistance**. The bacteria can be passed to humans by contact between flies and food, causing illnesses we can no longer easily treat. The results of his work highlight the dangers of using too many antibiotics on farm animals.

Flies can carry disease-causing bacteria on their feet and in their saliva.

Medical Entomologists at Work

Medical entomologists work on the role arthropods play in spreading diseases they carry, called vector-borne diseases. These account for 17 percent of infectious diseases and cause many deaths and serious illnesses around the world. Malaria and dengue fever are both tropical diseases that cause fever, vomiting, joint pain, and exhaustion, and can be deadly. They are passed on by biting mosquitoes. Other arthropods spread disease by carrying microbes from waste matter to our food, causing food poisoning. Medical entomologists ask questions about the role of arthropods in disease and how to tackle their spread.

*Scientists in Brazil release baby fish into a stream to feed on mosquito **larvae** and control the spread of dengue fever.*

LOOKING CLOSELY

An investigation is designed to collect data, such as measurements, counts, and readings. Many investigations begin with observation, either in the lab or in the field.

When the Field Is a Bog—or a Mountain

The "field" is anywhere research is carried out that is not in the laboratory. As arthropods live everywhere, this can be anywhere from a literal field of crops to a natural environment, such as a forest, swamp, mountain, or hedgerow. Or it could be a human-made environment, such as a house, bridge, or street.

An entomologist carries out careful field research in a meadow.

Looking Outdoors

In the field, entomologists observe arthropods in their natural habitats. They investigate how they interact with the environment and other animals, and they count or track populations. Medical entomologists often observe disease-carrying arthropods in their natural environment to study how they come into contact with humans. Discovering where and how they spend the different stages of their lives can help people come up with plans to remove or destroy them safely.

Looking Indoors

Other observations are carried out in the lab. This can involve close attention to certain types of behavior, such as observing how a biting insect feeds or how a spider spins a web. The entomologist might need to use a microscope to observe small arthropods or parts of arthropods.

An entomologist uses special equipment in the laboratory to investigate how a biting insect is attracted to the smell of his hand.

Taking Their Time

Some observations take just a few hours, but others can take many years. An entomologist studying how the number of arthropods changes has to collect data over a long period of time.

From the Field: Emmanuel Hakizimana

Emmanuel Hakizimana is a medical entomologist working in Rwanda in Africa. He figures out how common malaria-carrying mosquitoes are. Malaria is a major cause of death in Africa; it is caused by a parasite that is carried by mosquitoes. A mosquito picks up the parasite when it bites one person, and when it bites someone else, the parasite is transferred into that person's blood. Hakizimana's team trapped mosquitoes near village houses at night over three years. At the end of the period, the researchers killed and collected any remaining mosquitoes in the houses. They identified the type and tested them in a laboratory for infection with malaria. From the data, Hakizimana could work out the risk of malaria to people at different times of year and night.

TESTING TIMES

Experiments in entomology are often carried out in a laboratory. It's easier to control conditions such as temperature in the lab than in the field. Some experiments have to be done in the field, though. For example, an entomologist investigating how the introduction of a new predator affects the population of an arthropod will need to work in the animal's natural habitat. Investigations that begin in the lab might end with a field trial. A chemical to drive away moths would be developed in the lab, but then tested in the field to make sure it works under natural conditions.

Experimenting with arthropods in the lab means the animals have to be reared and cared for. Entomologists prepare food for their experimental subjects and keep them in suitable conditions.

Changing Mosquitoes

Genetic engineering is a branch of science that involves making changes to organisms by altering their **genetic** makeup. Entomologists use genetic engineering to change the inherited characteristics in arthropods.

Several dangerous diseases are spread by mosquitoes. Medical entomologists experiment with different ways of interrupting the way mosquitoes carry diseases between people. One method they try is to genetically change some mosquitoes, which they then release to breed with wild mosquitoes. One project makes the male mosquitoes infertile, so they can't breed successfully with females. Another changes the genes of mosquitoes so that the next generation will be unable to fly. These insects won't be able to bite people or breed as they can't fly to find a mate.

Entomologists Christopher Bamikole and Andrew Hammond work with genetically changed mosquitoes to try to stop the spread of disease.

From the Field: Fang (Rose) Zhu

Fang Zhu is a medical entomologist who works with bed bugs that have become resistant to the pesticides previously used to kill them. Her work is part of an international project investigating the genetics of bed bugs, and she plans to find the genes that give bed bugs resistance to pesticides. With this information, she hopes to find ways to work around the bugs' defenses. For example, bed bugs have adapted so that some pesticides pass straight through their gut without causing them harm. A solution might be to change the chemicals in the pesticide so that they are absorbed. Bed bugs don't cause diseases, but they bite people while they sleep, cause miserable itching, and are very difficult to get rid of. They are spreading around the world, often carried unknowingly by travelers in their luggage.

Bed bugs are tiny and hide during the day, making them difficult to remove.

TOOLS OF THE TRADE

Entomologists use a range of tools to collect data. Some are simple items used to catch, count, and measure arthropods in different ways. Others are sophisticated pieces of technology that collect data automatically, or help scientists to look closely at arthropods, or carry out complex procedures.

Sometimes It's Simple

Simple tools include nets for catching flying insects and sucking devices for picking up arthropods without touching them. To watch or catch arthropods that come out at night, entomologists can use light traps—the insects are attracted to a light and fly into a net. Entomologists also use many tools that other kinds of scientists use too, such as gloves, protective clothing, bottles to collect samples, **forceps**, and magnifying glasses.

An entomologist uses a modified leaf-blower to suck up and collect beetles.

Moths are attracted to light traps and are easily caught.

High-tech Tangles with Arthropods

Many entomologists use high-tech equipment. In the field, they can track swarms of insects using **GPS**, the same technology that a satellite navigation system in a car uses. They might use special cameras that respond to the heat released by living bodies, which reveals creatures hidden in the dark or underground. In the lab, entomologists use advanced tools for genetic engineering, high-power microscopes to examine arthropods in detail, and precise cutting tools to take arthropods' bodies apart and look inside them. They also use computers for imaging and modeling. For example, they might create a series of images of the inside of an arthropod's body with a scanner, or use software to work out when and where a swarm of pests is likely to form.

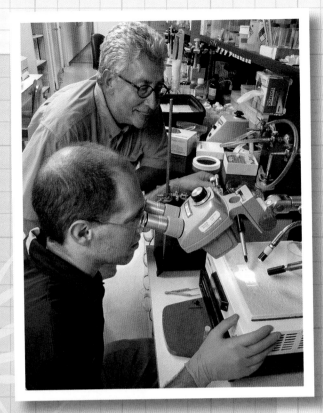

Microscopes help entomologists carry out detailed work—in this case, injecting a mosquito.

Zooming in on an image of an insect on the computer screen makes it easier to identify.

From the Field: Daniel Martin-Vega

Daniel Martin-Vega explores how maggots change into flies. He uses a small CT (computerized tomography) scanner to show the stage of development within a **pupa**. CT scanners build up a detailed image of the inside of a body from a series of X-rays taken at different angles. Martin-Vega is a forensic entomologist, helping the police solve crimes. He examines the eggs, maggots, pupae, and flies on dead bodies. His scanning work enables him to figure out what day an egg was laid. Different types of arthropods lay eggs in a body at different times after death, so Martin-Vega's expertise helps police find out when a person died.

FACTS FROM FINDINGS

Entomologists analyze and interpret their data so that they can draw conclusions and construct explanations. They often carry out calculations, compare new figures with previous data, look for patterns in the data, and construct computer models.

Working with Numbers

Entomologists often work with whole populations of organisms. They might investigate how changing a condition in the environment, such as the temperature or number of predators, affects the amount of arthropods. For this type of study, they need to compare the population before and after the change in conditions.

An entomologist analyzes mosquitoes in a secure lab.

Medical entomologists work with statistics (numerical data) that show arthropod populations and cases of illness. To find out how effective a pesticide is in preventing malaria, they would need to compare the number of mosquitoes and malaria cases in an area both with and without using the pesticide. They might use computer models to predict how quickly insects will reproduce. By changing conditions in the model, they can see the likely result if conditions in the real world changed in the same way.

A worker sprays pesticide to kill mosquitoes that carry dengue fever and zika virus. Entomologists will assess if the treatment is working.

Reflecting on Results

All scientists figure out whether their findings are significant (meaningful) or whether they could be produced by chance, or by some factor that they have not thought of or can't control. If an entomologist introduces a predator to eat insects that cause disease, and the disease becomes less common, they need to make sure the predator is really the reason for the change. Could a change in the weather, or some aspect of people's behavior, be affecting the rate of disease instead? Repeating tests, checking other conditions, and thinking through other possibilities are important parts of **verifying** scientific work.

There are many species of tick, and they spread several diseases. They represent a major public health risk.

From the Field: Marion Ripoche

Marion Ripoche works in Montréal, Canada, on Lyme disease caused by **ticks**. Lyme disease can cause a wide range of symptoms in humans, including muscle and joint pain. She uses data, recording tick bites and cases of infection to model the likely hot spots for the disease as it becomes more common. Ticks are major carriers of disease around the world, so her work will be useful elsewhere. As Lyme disease is relatively new to Canada, Ripoche can track and model it from its earliest stages.

SHARING FINDINGS

Scientists share their findings with each other and with the public. Sharing with peers allows other experts to check their work and make helpful suggestions. Other scientists can use the results in different areas, or develop a new study from the work. The whole scientific community benefits.

Ways of Sharing

Like other scientists, entomologists share their work by writing books and articles in scientific **journals** and talking at conferences. Articles are checked by peers to make sure that investigations used sound methods and were carried out properly, and that the conclusions are valid. All scientists follow the work of their peers, keeping up to date with their field.

Some entomologists bring their work to a wider audience. They give public lectures, appear at science fairs, work with museums, and make television programs. People come across arthropods every day, so it's important to help the public to understand which are dangerous and which are helpful, and how to live with and appreciate them.

Iraqi Girl Scouts learn about arthropods from a visiting entomologist.

From the Field: Bjoern von Reumont

Bjoern von Reumont studies how insects evolved. He works in water-filled, underground caves in Mexico looking for remipedes—arthropods that look like upside-down centipedes. Von Reumont has analyzed previous research that suggests insects developed from arthropods like centipedes. He is not convinced this is right, and asks whether insects might instead have evolved from crustaceans that live in the water. He has found that remipedes and insects have similar brains, nervous systems, and chemicals in their bodies. This suggests that they both evolved from the same ancestors. Another researcher, Bernhard Misof, has compared the genes of insects and remipedes to support von Reumont's idea.

An entomologist enters a water-filled underground cave in Mexico. Such investigations can be dangerous, as well as exciting.

Bringing Work Together

Journals publish many studies each year; most are based on a small area of research. Sometimes it is useful to bring together the results of many investigations. Studies that do this are called metastudies. They don't involve new research with arthropods, but work with results that have been shared. For example, a metastudy of research into insect damage to crops in a region can compare information from many studies. One such metastudy has found that growing mixed crops or changing crops led to less insect damage than growing one crop all the time.

WORKING TOGETHER: THE BIGGER PICTURE

Most scientists work in large teams, often collaborating (working together) with others in different countries. Arthropods move around as the climate changes, so it's increasingly important for entomologists to share their expertise worldwide.

An entomologist in Minnesota sorts through mosquitoes collected by colleagues in a large-scale project employing many experts.

A World of Information

New species of arthropods are discovered all the time, but entomologists have to check that what they have found is actually new. Large databases of arthropods from all over the world provide a useful way of checking. Keeping these up to date is an international effort that benefits entomologists worldwide.

Beyond Biology

No scientist works in a bubble. Entomologists often work with other biologists, investigating how arthropods interact with other living things, such as plants, birds, or mammals. Their work can also be used in public health, medical research, engineering, and crime solving. Shared findings from research can be used by experts in any field, and entomologists are often involved in projects that span more than one type of science.

From the Field: Paul Stamets and Steve Sheppard

Arthropods can spread disease in other animals, and even in other arthropods. Since 1987, honey bees have been attacked by a type of mite that spreads viral disease, causing "colony collapse"—the death of many bees in a hive. Bee expert Steve Sheppard noticed that bees that eat a certain fungus rarely suffer colony collapse. He teamed up with mycologist (fungus expert) Paul Stamets to investigate whether chemicals from the fungus can protect bees. In their experiments, they put fungus into the bees' diet and hives and collect data on levels of disease in the bee colonies. This research brings together expertise in different fields to tackle a problem in entomology.

Putting Results to Work

Medical entomologists work with public health officials to prevent disease. Together, they figure out where to use pesticides to kill arthropods that carry disease, and where to look out for the diseases they cause. Arthropods don't always behave in the way computer models predict. Unexpected factors can affect an arthropod's distribution, such as competition with other animals or new food sources or predators.

Entomologists work in a 160-foot (50-meter) long beehive to examine how bees react to chemicals used on rapeseed crops.

A GROWING FIELD

Arthropods are very important to all ecosystems and have considerable impact on how people live. There is still plenty to discover about these fascinating creatures.

Expanding Threats

Climate change is altering the distribution of arthropods, and they are also easily moved around by people. Just a few beetles or flies on a plane can cross the world in hours. They can travel in tourists' luggage or in **cargo**. Sometimes, they end up in an area where they can survive. They colonize new environments and might spread diseases, harm local plants, or damage local arthropod populations. It is more important than ever that entomologists share their experience and research worldwide.

Putting Arthropods to Use

Arthropods have always broken down waste material from plants and animals. Humans now produce a lot of waste that's hard to deal with. Some researchers are looking at whether arthropods could play a part in removing plastic waste, which could otherwise lie around for thousands of years. A type of wax-moth caterpillar has been found to eat plastic bags. Entomologists might be able to breed colonies of caterpillars to help us tackle this environmental threat.

An entomologist measures the amount of plastic broken down by a wax-moth caterpillar.

Get Involved

It's never too early to become an **amateur** entomologist. There are arthropods all around us, and you can study them without leaving your own area. Take care, though: Some arthropods can sting or bite, and in some parts of the world, they can be dangerous. Avoid touching arthropods directly as you might damage them, or they might hurt you.

It is possible to investigate arthropods using simple and cheap tools, such as plastic boxes, tweezers, and a magnifying glass.

You can often see displays of arthropods at zoos and natural history museums. You can learn about them at these venues or from videos and books. There are "citizen-science" projects you can become involved with, too. These invite members of the public to help in real scientific research. You might do some hands-on observation, such as counting and recording arthropods in your area. Or you might work with computer data that have been put online for processing by the public (see page 30).

Some very important work has been done by amateur entomologists. Entomology is one of the areas of biology in which it is easy to get started on your own—you don't have to fly to an exotic location or have access to a high-tech lab.

PROJECT: NATURE'S RECYCLERS

Arthropods play a vital role recycling natural waste. They do it everywhere and all the time. You can investigate a part of it.

Ask a Question

There are many types of waste. Think of questions that you can ask about how arthropods break waste down. Do different arthropods break down different materials? Do adults or larvae break down waste? How quickly do they get to work?

Investigate!

You will investigate how arthropods break down different types of food waste. You will need the following equipment:

- Three different kinds of natural waste, such as meat or pet food, soft fruit, some cooked rice, pasta, or potatoes

- Four disposable, transparent, waterproof containers, such as plastic takeout boxes

- A sharp knife or pointed scissors

- Magnifying glass

- Measuring cup and spoon

- Camera

You will investigate if there are differences in how and when arthropods colonize and break down the different foods.

Follow These Steps:

1 With the help of an adult, make small holes in the sides of each box so that flying or crawling insects can get in.

2 Measure one type of waste and place in one of the boxes. Repeat with the other types of waste, using the same amount. Leave one box empty as a **control**.

3 Place the boxes outside, somewhere sheltered so that they don't blow away.

4 Observe them over at least two to four weeks, checking them each day. Use a magnifying glass to look carefully, but don't open the boxes. Can you see arthropods? What kinds? Can you see eggs? Can you see maggots? How long does it take before eggs hatch or maggots become pupae? What comes from the pupae?

5 Draw or photograph what you see each day; count eggs, maggots, pupae, adult arthropods; and try to distinguish between types, even if you can't identify them.

6 At the end of your study, throw away the boxes without opening them.

Food waste attracts many kinds of arthropods.

Forming Conclusions

Did you see different arthropods on different foods? How many did you count on each? When did they arrive? How quickly did they colonize the food? Some of the foods might have grown mold. Did you see any arthropods on the mold? How long did it take for each type of arthropod to go from egg, to pupa, to adult? Did the adults stay in the box or leave? What conclusions can you draw about how different arthropods work with rotting matter?

Make a poster or presentation of your findings. You might be able to include tables or charts and pictures of the arthropods you saw.

LEARNING MORE

BOOKS

Burns, Loree Griffin, and Ellen Harasimowicz. *Beetle Busters: A Rogue Insect and the People Who Track It* (Scientists in the Field) HMH Books for Young Readers, 2018.

Burns, Loree Griffin, and Ellen Harasimowicz. *The Hive Detectives: Chronicle of a Honey Bee Catastrophe* (Scientists in the Field). HMH Books for Young Readers, 2013.

Koontz, Robin Michal. *Entomologists*. Rourke Publishing Group, 2015.

Montgomery, Sy and Nic Bishop. *The Tarantula Scientist* (Scientists in the Field Series). HMH Books for Young Readers, 2007.

Murawski, Darlyne, and Nancy Honovich. *Ultimate Bugopedia: The Most Complete Bug Reference Ever*. National Geographic Kids, 2013.

Pomeroy, Sarah B., and Jeyaraney Kathirithamby. *Maria Sibylla Merian: Artist, Scientist, Adventurer*. Harry N. Abrams, 2018.

Spilsbury, Louise, and Richard Spilsbury. *Insect Investigators: Entomologists* (InfoSearch: Scientists at Work). Heinemann Library, 2008.

PLACES TO VISIT

Many large cities have a natural history museum or a zoo. These often have displays or information about arthropods and the work of entomologists. Some have special butterfly displays in the summer where you can see the butterflies and their caterpillars and pupae up close.

Universities and colleges frequently take part in or host public science fairs and festivals where you can find out about the work of entomologists and learn about their research projects.

ONLINE

http://studentsdiscover.org/lesson/ category/citizen-science/
Has citizen-science projects and suggestions for investigations specifically for students.

https://monarchlab.org/mlmp
A long-term citizen-science project in the USA to monitor monarch butterflies. Find butterfly larvae in your area and report them.

www.naba.org/butter_counts.html
Take part in a butterfly count throughout North America and Mexico.

www.inaturalist.org
Take photos of arthropods you find and contribute to science—and have help identifying them.

www.zooniverse.org
Lists a range of citizen-science projects, including some in entomology.

http://content.yardmap.org
Take part in a project to provide, track, and protect habitats for wildlife in North America.

www.environmentalscience.org/career/ entomologist
Find out what it takes to become an entomologist and what entomologists do.

GLOSSARY

amateur Nonprofessional; someone who engages in an activity from interest rather than to earn a living

biology The study of living organisms, including plants, animals, fungi, and microorganisms

cargo Goods that are carried by ship, train, or other means of transport

classify Put into groups or categories by choosing characteristics that distinguish between organisms

climate change Change in the long-term patterns of weather experienced in a particular region or the whole world; currently leading to higher temperatures and altered patterns of winds, rain, and storms around the world

control A subject or sample in an experiment that is not exposed to any of the changes the experiment is trying out; kept as an untreated example so that researchers can be certain any changes in other samples are caused by their treatment

crustacean A type of arthropod with a hard, jointed external skeleton. Many crustaceans live in water, such as crabs and crayfish

data Raw facts and figures collected from observations and measurements

ecology Part of biology that focuses on how organisms interact with their environment and with each other

ecosystem An environment and all the organisms it contains

environmental science The study of the environment, how it changes, how parts of it interact, and how environmental problems might be solved; it brings together many different kinds of science, including biology, chemistry, physics, geology (the science of rocks), and hydrology (the science of water systems)

evolution The process by which organisms change over time

evolve To adapt over time, changing form or behavior to suit new conditions or a changing environment

forceps An instrument for grasping, holding, or pulling on things

genetic Relating to genes and inherited characteristics

GPS The Global Positioning System that uses satellites going around Earth to track objects or organisms from place to place

habitat The place in which an organism lives

journal A publication that presents articles written by experts on scientific or other academic topics

larva/larvae (adj. **larval**) First stage of an arthropod's life after it has hatched from an egg; maggots and caterpillars are examples of larvae

microbe A microorganism; an organism so small that it can only be seen through a microscope

mite Very small eight-legged arthropod related to spiders

model A copy of an object or situation that can be used to examine, study, or experiment in place of working with the original; often mathematical or computer-based mimics of situations in which a scientist can try out different conditions, such as changing the temperature or the population of an organism, and use a model to predict what other changes are likely to result

naturalist A person who studies the natural world—living organisms and their environments

organism A living thing of any type: animal, plant, fungus, or microorganism

parasite An organism that lives in or on another (its host), bringing no benefit to the host and often causing it harm

pollinate Carry pollen from one plant to another, fertilizing the second plant by introducing pollen (the male sex cells) to combine with the female sex cells of the plant so that it can produce seeds

pupa Stage between a larva (maggot or caterpillar) and an adult when the arthropod builds a cocoon around itself and changes its form while inside it

resistance The ability to withstand hostile conditions, including the ability of organisms to withstand poisons or other methods of trying to destroy them

robotics The study and use of automated devices, programmed or controlled from a distance to carry out tasks

species A distinct type of organism, genetically distinct from other types

termite An insect like an ant that lives in huge communities of millions of individuals and builds large mounds or towers from earth

tick A small eight-legged arthropod that burrows into the flesh of animals

vector An animal that carries a disease infecting other organisms

verifying Making sure that something is true and accurate

INDEX

ABOUT THE AUTHOR

Anne Rooney is a full-time writer, specializing in books on science and technology, and the history of science, for young people and adults. Her main interests are evolution and other aspects of the biological sciences, and she writes frequently on these topics. In 2018 she was shortlisted for the Royal Society Young Person's Book Prize.